What Cootchie Wash Do You Use?

13 Life Lessons and Real-Life Advice Learned from Online Dating

By: Wendi M. Davis

ISBN: 978-1-7364231-0-3

Acknowledgements

This book would not have been possible without the love and support of my husband, Ryan, who also served as my developmental editor. Words cannot express my gratitude to my friend, Natalie, who was my sounding board throughout the entire process of writing this book. And, lastly, I would like to thank my boys, Aidan and Logan, who each, in their own unique way, encouraged me to keep writing every day. I love you all.

Table of Contents

How Did It All Begin?

Let me start by introducing myself. My name is Wendi. I am a mother of two that also happens to juggle a full-time, demanding career. To set the stage, I was divorced, single and not really ready to mingle. But now that I am 41 and newly married, I wanted to share with you some of the things I learned from my online dating journey, in hopes, that it will shorten your own.

Let's start at the beginning. I never really dated much in high school until I met my then-boyfriend when I was in tenth grade and I thought I found my soulmate at the ripe age of 16. SPOILER ALERT: I was wayyyy wrong. I went on to marry my high school sweetheart at the age of 24 and of course, you can guess it.... a house and two kids quickly followed. Fast-forward to the age of 32, where I found myself divorced with two kids and no idea how to date.

The word itself brought fear to me, not to mention that I never even thought I would be facing this scenario again in my lifetime. But I guess we are all guilty of having this thought when we are with someone who we think we will be with forever. So, at this point in my life and at a ripe, young age of 32, I really didn't have much dating experience. I mean seriously: I met a boy then we were together for a long time and that was pretty much the extent of my dating history. Well, I dated one other person during a brief break I had with my high school sweetheart when I was twenty-one. But enough about that…you get what I am saying here.

Picture this: I was laying on the couch for six months and every day my friend, Betsy, kept pushing me to get off the couch and stressing that it was time for me to start dating. I had no clue how to even meet people given that I had been off the market for so long nor did I even have the desire to start doing it. But she kept pushing and then uttered the dreaded words of ONLINE DATING. Eeek, wait, what?!? Online dating…isn't this where serial killers find you? I wasn't sure if I even wanted to go out on that big, scary limb but I knew that I had no idea how meet people any other way.

In this book, we will talk about the lessons I learned from online dating and real-life advice based on where my experiences took me and what I learned along the way. Don't think this is going to be the type of book where I am talking at you the whole time. Oh, no. I am going to ask you to do some internal reflections of your own and write down your thoughts along the way. You will need to make sure you have your Cootchie Wash Recipe Book or simply have a pad of paper, journal or a notebook and pen nearby as you are reading this book. I will explain why this is important later. Let's get started.

The Dreaded Six-Letter Word - Dating: Do I Have To Do It?

Dating.... the dreaded 6-letter word. The word itself can bring on a host of feelings and emotions when you hear it. For some, it may strike fear that causes a bout of anxiety. For others, it brings about terrifyingly horrible thoughts about their own past experiences or experiences that they may have read or heard about that happened to others.

For me, it was a lot of both! I knew I was not alone because this is something that all women struggle with at some point in their lifetime. It doesn't matter if you are 20, 40 or 60. It doesn't matter if you have always been single, divorced or widowed. We all have had to face this word and all that it entails a time or two in our journey.

Do you remember my friend, Betsy? I mentioned her earlier, she was the one who was pushing me to get off the couch after six months. She literally came to my house every day and kept talking about how it was time...time to start dating...meeting people, etc. You know... what your "coupled" friends always tell you when you are freshly (or not so freshly) single. Anyway, we all need a Betsy in our lives because truth be told, I probably would still be laying on that same couch today if it wasn't for her (figuratively speaking of course).

Betsy is the type of friend that would go out to bars with me even though she didn't drink; she did it because it was getting me off the couch and out of house. She was also the friend who helped me take pictures for my online profile and helped come up with answers to the gazillion questions you are asked to fill out when you create a profile on a dating app. She, finally, had me all set up to start dating online even though I was kicking and screaming all the way there. Little did I know, this was about to become one of the best and worst things that ever happened to me.

Even though I begrudgingly agreed to create a profile, I was still not convinced that I would go out on an actual date. You know I was still thinking that online dating was the way serial killers found you. And, before you think it.... Yes, I know there are some stories of bad things that happened to people that were dating online, but by normal standards, this was irrational thinking. I cannot stress enough that the thought of online dating was scary and plain, foreign to me. Not only did I have little dating experience, but I was also nervous about the idea of meeting someone online. I told myself that they could be lying about who they are. I was not even considering the fact that people lie about who they are all the time....IN-PERSON.

Lets' be honest, I was still emotionally stuck on my last relationship. I was struggling with figuring out how to be alone, convincing myself I wasn't going to hell for divorcing my husband, raising two boys as a single mother, the list went on and on. You know... the list of things we cling to and repeat over and over to ourselves until those thoughts are the only thoughts that go through our head.

Life Lesson# 1- It's okay to be stuck on a past relationship, just don't live there too long

No one can tell you how long is the "right" amount of time to grieve a past relationship. But one thing is for sure… you can't live there forever! I had "my" Betsy to keep pushing me and making sure I didn't get stuck there.

A question to ask yourself: Who is your Betsy? Do you have that person who will give you time to grieve but will also know when it is time to push you out of your comfort zone? If not, you need to find one ASAP!

I slowly got it out of my head and started to accept the fact that I could overcome all of the things that I was worried about and that maybe Betsy was right… it was time to start meeting people and taking the next step in my life. After about a month, I finally decided to make my profile public. OMG! I can't believe I ACTUALLY took the step to do it! As I clicked the button and sat there wondering what would happen next. BAM! Within .05 nanoseconds, my notifications were going off. What was all of this craziness? At this point, feelings of nervousness and excitement came over me. Do I respond?

How do I respond? Who are these people? Is it really this easy? I was shocked by how quickly I started receiving messages. I immediately called Betsy and she came over to my house within minutes (she just lived a few houses down from me).

She started looking at people's profiles and saying oh, this one is cute or that one has a good job. Little did I know that these guys were getting notifications when she… or should I say when "I" looked at their profiles. Let's just say that led to repeat contact from them. Ugh. I was becoming overwhelmed by what was happening and uh oh… what is this feeling that was starting to creep up? It was guilt. Why in the world am I feeling like this… Guilt like I was cheating… OMG, what is wrong with me? Why am I am feeling this way? I am divorced… what gives? In reality, I had to process through all of my unresolved feelings to understand that I wasn't cheating and realize that I had no reason to feel guilty whatsoever. And, once I did that, that is when the fun began for me… or so I thought.

Let me tell you, I was on a high responding to all the messages that I received. It made me feel pretty and wanted. I was starting to experience all of those artificial things we think we want or need to hear. Wow, this is easy, I thought. I was just lying on the couch watching tv and talking to men. My boys were none the wiser that I was talking to other men besides their father. This is GREAT! And those were my famous last thoughts that led me to actually taking the next step and that was to start going out on dates. Real, actual, in-person dates!

INGREDIENT REFLECTION: Sit quietly for a few minutes and honestly think about if there is anything you are still holding on to that no longer serves you. Now, write them down on your paper or in your Recipe Book. Now, think about why you are holding on to these negative things and what you can do to release them. Write this list down next to each "thing" that no longer serves you.

Online-Palooza: Should I Even Ask?

When I finally made the decision to begin online dating… let's just say I went all in! Even though I found talking to these people from my couch rather easy, a change was starting to happen in my life and I had to change with it… or so I thought. The change that occurred in my life was that my boys started going to their fathers' house every other weekend. That's when my next emotional roller coaster started. This is when I really started to struggle with the concept of being alone. I mean seriously, I didn't know what to do with myself. I had always had family around or a significant other or my kids. I had never experienced this feeling before.

This made me start thinking about all the times I would see single people or people who I thought were single, out and about. I would see these people go to the movies by themselves, restaurants, casinos… you name it. As time went on, I started to notice them more and more. But I knew I was not confident enough to do any of those things A-L-O-N-E. So much for the fake, inflated self-esteem I thought I had from receiving all of those messages on the dating app. POOF… it was gone.

In the stillness, I was left with my broken, insecure, emotional self that I wasn't ready to face yet. So, instead of dealing with it, I jumped no-holds bar into the dating scene. Before I get into it, I want to say that I am telling you this not because I am proud of what I did but so, maybe, it will help you avoid doing it. I was busy working my 9-5 job and being a full-time parent of two boys which also included juggling all of the sporting events and homework assignments that occurred during the week by myself. While all of this was keeping me busy, I knew that the dreaded "alone" weekend would enviably arrive. There I would be in a quiet, empty house; afraid to be left alone with my thoughts and myself. So, I started to avoid it at all costs and that is when I started my own version of speed-dating.

The first couple of dates were awkward. I didn't know how to make small talk nor did I really have any interest in truly opening myself up or learning about the other person sitting across from me. In all honesty, this revelation didn't come to me until a little further down my "dating road." But, once I had a couple of these "fake dates" as I called them under my belt, that's when I became what I now refer to as the "One Date Queen." On the weekends my boys left to be with their father, I would have already lined up 2 dates on Friday night, 3 dates on Saturday and 2-3 on Sunday (depending on what time the boys were coming home). I literally used this as a way to stay busy and no, I am not proud of it. I feel bad for the men I went out with during this time. And, no, I wasn't some type of hoe-bag either. I would meet them for lunch, dinner, or drinks. We would talk for an hour or two and then I would give them a quick hug and a promise of a second date that would never materialize.

I soon found myself needing to figure out a way to remember the names of all of these men since I had fully embraced the

Wendi-style of speed dating. At this point in time, I had joined several online dating apps. So, once I started talking to these men outside of the app, I would have to create fake names for them in my phone just to remember who they were and which app I met them on. I got it down to a science. Let's say I was meeting John from the ABC dating app. I would use his first name and something we talked about in the "first name" slot of the contact card in my phone and then I would put the name of the app we met on as his last name. That way, when we texted or met up, I would know that I was talking to or meeting: John-has three dogs ABC app. It made for an easy conversation starter too because I could start talking about whatever I listed as the "thing to remember him by". This was the only way I could figure out how to keep them straight and not end up looking like I didn't know who I was talking to. It became a job in and of itself.

Let's just say that I quickly got the hang of this online dating thing. You would think that I would have been nervous when meeting a new person for the first time, most people would be. But no, not me. I would walk in to meet my date and talk with the utmost confidence during our meal but by the end of the night as I walked away from my last date, the dread of the empty house would start to haunt me. That's when I would reach out to one of my friends to go out with me and close the bars down. Here enters my friend, Charity. Poor, Charity. To this day, she swears she still has PTSD (post-traumatic stress disorder) from those nights.

Charity was also recently divorced and so, in my mind, she was the perfect person for me to reach out to for my next charade.

I would call her and beg her to go have a couple of drinks with me, but she knew what would really happen. Charity would fuss and cuss at me, but she would always (eventually) agree to go out for "a little bit." That "little bit" always turned into too many drinks, lots of dancing, closing down the bars then late-night drives through White Caste with her drunken friend ordering a red pop and five cheeseburger sliders, that she never finished.

Life Lesson #2- Learn to be comfortable with yourself in the silence

The life lesson here is one that took me years to learn and I hope you are able to learn it faster than I did! Let me be clear, I am not saying you must learn to go the movies or restaurants by yourself. Listen, I still won't do those things alone. No, it's not because I am insecure or have any other issue that I haven't dealt with. The bottom line is… I don't like it nor do I want to do. So, I don't and that's okay. What I am saying here is that you need to process through your emotions and become more self-aware. You can do this by finding a healthy way to deal with your issues that is right for you. Maybe that is talking to a therapist, a close friend or family member. Or, maybe, it is finding a new hobby that you enjoy. For me, it became walking trails at the local metro parks. Sometimes, I would hike the trails with my friend, Charity. Other times, I would go by myself. The quiet, serene surroundings left me with my thoughts even though I was, technically, in public. This quiet time taught me how to be alone with my thoughts and myself and to be comfortable with that. The more often I went, the more I learned to be alone and absorb the silence and slowly, over time, I learned to enjoy the time alone with myself and not be concerned with anything or anyone else.

Trust me, if you do this… "your" Charity and your liver will thank you!

INGREDIENT REFLECTION: What is missing in your life, right now? What void(s) are you trying to fill? What positive activities can you start doing to fill the void(s)? Write your responses down and go back to them as often as you need to as you work through your internal processes.

What the What?

Let's pause for a moment and talk about some of the crazy stories that either I or some of my friends (both male and female) have experienced while dating online. If you are a "more seasoned" online dater, you will be able to relate to these and maybe even add a few more experiences to my list. If you are new to online dating, use these stories as a guide of what to expect when you first venture out into the crazy world of online dating.

Numero uno.... Ladies, put your hands up if you have ever received the infamous d*#k pic!?! I can see all of you "seasoned" online daters raising your hands now and nodding furiously an overwhelming YESSS! OMG, I mean SERIOIUSLY!?!? I can't even count how many penises I have seen at this point; in every shape, size and color. It is ABSOLUTELY insane at the rate these bad boys come flying into your inbox. Guys, SPOILER ALERT! They are not cute...I REPEAT... they are not cute! At times, it would get so bad that I would get to the point of making my profile private because I would get so many of them in my inbox that I couldn't stand it any longer. And just to be clear, I had to do this more than once.

Come on, guys! Do you really think that is what we want to see? They must think so. I swear men just assume we are visual creatures like them. They think when we see it, we will just want to jump on them! Get out of here with all of that, man! But there must be a percentage of times where this works. Otherwise, I would think (or hope) that they would stop doing it. UGH! Bottom line here, ladies: if you receive these type of pictures.... hit Delete! I mean delete and block with the quickness. No need to waste our time and energy on these types of guys.

While we are on this subject, there have also been instances where guys have even taken it to the next level. Have you ever experienced going from having a normal conversation to suddenly, a video pops up? You think wow, that's weird. I warn you now! DO NOT OPEN IT! I repeat... DO NOT OPEN IT! Nine times out of ten, it will be a video of a man masturbating. Yes, you heard me right. Yep, that's exactly what we want to see right after asking what their favorite hobby is. NOT!!! Ladies, delete now. Do not move forward. Take this as a sign that he is not the man for you.

I have another doozy for you. Have you ever been the recipient of va-jay pictures? Now, I know that I clearly marked that I am heterosexual on my profile. And yes, I double-checked it just to make sure it read: Woman Seeking Man. But, yep, you guessed it... I ended up receiving pictures of boobs and va-jays from women who were pretending to be men on the site. Listen, I am all for love is love. And I am not judging others here. But I know I am heterosexual. And no, I can't be convinced otherwise. So, thanks but no thanks.

Ok, I mentioned in the beginning of this book that I started this online thing in my early 30's and continued to into my early 40's. I posted professional pictures of myself on my profile. By professional, no, I don't mean photos I paid for. I mean pictures of myself dressed in work suits and other tasteful clothing. So, believe me when I tell you, I was utterly shocked when I received my first (yes, I said FIRST) request for someone to be my sugar daddy. Ummm, excuse me?!? The first one made me question my profile: is it something I am wearing, is it something I said in my profile? The answer was no, but it still made me wonder. Nonetheless, you know what I am going to say here.... DELETE.

However, after about the fifth time I received one, I became curious and wanted to ask a question about it. Yes, curiosity got the best of me... we are all human, right?!? The man who just happened to send this particular message to me was an older gentleman who was a farmer and lived about 30 minutes away from me. And before you ask... yes, I looked at his profile. So, I decided to ask him, "What does this entail exactly?" He replied. "You and your boys (I said I had two boys on my profile) would come and live with me on the farm. I pay someone to clean the house so you wouldn't need to worry about doing any of that. And, I have a Lexus SUV for you to drive." And, yes, pictures of the house, farm and vehicle were included. Don't think it didn't cross my mind for just a split second... ohh, that sounds niiiiceee. It was only for a fleeting second, so don't judge me! But, in all reality, I could not nor would I ever actually consider doing that. But I had to know what the ask entailed, right?!?! Needless to say, the response was a no thank you and DELETE.

Now, this is where those professional pictures bit me in the arse. I started receiving a lot and I mean A LOT of messages from 20-something guys. Flattered, sure! But knowing I would never allow anything really serious to happen with them, I would respond nicely (because my mommy side kicked in). I would say something along the lines of: I am old enough to be your mother or that they needed to find someone their own age, etc. Nevertheless, I would always have a couple of them try to keep pushing the issue and eventually they would ask if I wanted to be their sugar momma or be like Stella and get my groove back. Boy, please! I am already raising two boys and I don't need another one to take care of. So much for trying to be nice....DELETE!

I also received a handful of messages from couples looking for a third person to join their want-to-be menage-a-trois. I was truly shocked by how many of these requests I received. Let me explain how these types of messages happen. The man (or so I thought) would reach out to me and send the first message and engage in small talk for a few lines then BOOM! They would drop the bomb. Yes, I mean "they". All of a sudden, a picture of their wife or girlfriend would pop up and she would start messaging and asking me to join them in their want-to-be love triangle. Wait, what? I am not judging anyone's lifestyle choices here, but no... that is not my thing. So, my answer was no... I will take a pass. Thanks though!

If those stories weren't enough for you. Just wait until you hear some of the in-person interactions we are going to talk about next. We have all heard about catfishing, right? I have never experienced this firsthand, but my friends have told me horror stories of people using other people's pictures that do not even resemble the person they were supposedly meeting. When they showed up looking for the person that they thought they were meeting, some strange-looking being would be waving them over to a table. I am not being superficial here but come on! We all have things that we are attracted to. So, why delay the inevitable?!? When this would happen, nine times out of ten, my friends would go ahead and oblige the person by having the lunch, dinner, or drinks with them. They would quickly bolt after that and never contact that person again. I don't blame them!

Along this same line, one of my friends told me a story about one of her dates that turned disastrous. She had a rule for herself when it came to waiting on a potential date to show up at a restaurant and that was for her to only wait 10 minutes for them to show up. Well, in the story I am getting ready to tell you, this particular guy didn't show up until 30 minutes later! Why did she wait so long? A group of her friends ended up walking into the same restaurant and saw her waiting to be seated. Of course, they asked her what she was doing there. She gave them the standard line that she waiting on one of her friends who was running late. So, at this point, she was committed. When the gentleman (I use that term lightly) finally showed up, the server seated them right next to her group of friends. (I will come back to this part of the story a little later.) At this point, she is thinking that it couldn't get any worse, but just wait… it does. Let me set the stage for why it went downhill fast (beside the fact the dude showed up 30 minutes late). We talked earlier about folks using other people's photos, but we never mentioned folks lying about their height. Ok, a couple of inches one way or another… Okay, I get that.

I mean I have been using the same weight on my driver's license since I was 20. But that's a whole different story.

This man had put on his profile that he was 5'10. In all seriousness, he was about 4'9" and that was on a good day with high-soled boots on. I am not judging his height here but come onnnnn people. Let's try to keep it within reason. What measuring system was he using? Metric? Not to mention, he also was a very angry person and that characteristic showed through over and over during their dinner. So, not only did he fail to declare his elf-like status, but the fact that he was an angry elf took it to a whole other level.

Now, circling back to her group of friends, they witnessed all of this unfolding and she was sure that they even felt the uncomfortableness that was oozing from her table. She really didn't want to have to face her friends after they witnessed her dating debacle. But guess what? When she did see them again, they never brought it up to her! So, the moral of this story is: if you see this happening to someone you know, be like this group of friends and know that this is "the thing" that shall never be mentioned again!

While we are on the subject of dinner, let me tell you about a dinner date that happened to a male counterpart of mine who was just trying out online dating for the first time. I mean this was his first dinner EVER with someone from an online dating app and it was their first-time meeting in-person. They decided to meet at a steakhouse for dinner. His date started out as you would expect… with some small talk and then it was time to place their order.

When the food arrived, this is where it all went downhill… really quickly! After the food arrived, he noticed that his date wasn't eating her dinner. So, he asked her if there was something wrong with her food. She replied no and that she was saving it to take it home to her young son. He then said, "Go ahead and eat your food, I will order something for you to take back to him." Even after he made that offer, she still didn't really eat anything… she just picked at it. She then asked, out of the blue, "Do you just want to pack up your clothes now?" He chuckled and asked what she meant by that. She proceeded to ask (with a straight face), "Do you just want to go pack up your clothes and move in with me and be my sons' dad?" The waitress (who was in ear shot) heard what was just asked of him and she shot him a look of horror as if she was saying: RUN, DUDE, RUN with her eyes. She then hurriedly brought his check over to him and said I can close you out now if you would like. And he quickly handed over the money and said, "Keep the change!" Needless to say, that date was a one and done.

The last story I want to tell you about comes with a purpose and that is to remind you to set rules for yourself when it comes to online dating and stick to them. My number one rule was to never meet up with someone I just started messaging. I wanted to give it a few days to make sure they weren't some type of stalker or something. Well, one night I was bored and the boys weren't home so I broke my cardinal rule. And boy, did I pay for it!

It was around 9:00 pm on a Friday night when I started messaged with someone new. He mentioned that he was going to be close to the area of town that I lived in and asked if I wanted to grab a quick drink. And, like I said, I was bored so I said yes. I quickly started to regret that decision as soon as we met at the bar. As soon as I arrived, I got a funny feeling in my stomach, but I ignored it. I told myself that I was just being weird about the situation because it was out of my normal comfort zone. After the first drink, the man became increasingly forceable with the same request: let's leave, grab some beers and go back to your house. The man was being so forceful about it that when he went to the restroom, the bouncer walked over to me and asked me if I was okay. I assured him that I was fine and that I would not be leaving with the man. To make a long story short, my response to his repeated question was "Umm, nooo Mc Crazy... I don't think so." I told him he should leave soon because there was still time to go to another bar and maybe he could find a hoe bag there to take him home. He finally decided to leave. I stayed in the bar until I saw him drive away...in the opposite direction of my house. Whew, that was a close one.

Life Lesson #3: Red flags ARE red flags.... Believe them when you see or feel them

These were just a few cases that I wanted to use to help you identify some red flags. But I also wanted to use these stories to demonstrate a deeper point. Red flags can be glaring and right in your face or they may be subtle. Either way, don't ignore them. Take action immediately so that you won't have to pay for it in the long run.

I know that was a lot to take in. Hang in there. It does get better...I promise.

INGREDIENT REFLECTION: Be really honest with yourself here. Do you ignore red flags when you see or feel them? If so, why do you think you continuously repeat this behavior?

Man-ifesting... What?

Now that we have the horror stories out of the way. Let's keep it moving. At this point, I am almost a year into my online dating experience. I have calmed down on scheduling dates and I am only going out once or twice a week at this point. I am feeling better about myself and my single status. Little did I know that things were getting ready to change (AGAIN).

I am sure we all have experienced the having "too many" glasses of wine with friends or driving around with your friends with the windows rolled down singing or otherwise, as seen by others, screaming at the top of your lungs songs like "Since you have been gone" or "Stronger" by Kelly Clarkson or some other female-led ballad that exemplifies female strength and independence. Those were just the ones that Charity and I used during our escapades. I am sure you and your friends may be guilty of doing this a time or two. These are just some of the things we do as part of our lady tribe rituals. We do these things to make us feel connected to each other, to make us feel better about ourselves and/or our situations and that is okay! With that being said, Charity and I had planned to have one of our drinking (too much) wine around a fire night. But little did I know, that would end up changing my online dating experience even though I didn't realize it at the time.

Let me back up for a minute because I realized that I didn't give you a description of my friend, Charity, and this is important for understanding the context of what I am getting ready to talk about in this chapter. I used to call Charity my "woo-woo" friend. She was into creating vision boards and manifesting dreams and goals. She always had a positive outlook on life and was constantly trying to get me to read books that I had no interest in reading.

Back to the story, here we are sitting around the fire, drinking our wine and she says, "Wendi, you need to write down what you are looking for in a man!" In my head, I am already thinking, here we go again with the "woo-woo" stuff. But I appeased her and agreed to make a list. She quickly grabbed a pad of paper and pen and off I went. The list below wasn't my first list, but I don't have a copy of it any longer and I will explain why a little later in this chapter.

The List of What I Wanted in a Man:
Provider
Security
Respected
Fun
Spontaneous
Planner
Driven
Loyal
Faithful
Honorable
Handsome

Energy
Successful
Wealthy
Financially Responsible
Loving
Caring
Open
Honest
Passionate
Great in Bed
Dependable
Family-Oriented
I want to feel like I am the only woman in the world!

After I wrote my list, Charity told me to take it home and put it somewhere safe… in a place that I would remember. When I got home, I did just that and placed it in my Bible. In all honesty, after I put it in my Bible, I completely forgot about it. From that point forward, my online dating life became a bit more meaningful as I started to find myself in longer-lasting relationships. I ended up having three relationships that each lasted about 1 ½ -2 years each. The interesting thing about this was that each one of the relationships taught me a valuable life lesson.

Life Lesson #4: You don't need a man (or woman) in your life, you just want one - Know the difference

My first serious relationship from online dating, was an interesting one. This relationship lasted about one and half years. Throughout this time, the person worked second shift and I worked first. I really didn't think much of the fact that we worked different schedules. However, ultimately, this led me to some deep insights about myself and the relationship. Let me start by saying that even though I am all womanpower, hear me roar... there were still things I thought I needed a man to do. I believed I needed a man to fix things, take out the trash, mow the lawn, change light bulbs, etc. I know, I know...how 1950's of me. Anyway, back to the story.

As the relationship grew, I would ask my partner to take care of these things for me. He would always say that I could do them for myself or tell me to find someone to call to do the repairs because he would be working. After several of these conversations, the light bulb clicked in my head (no pun intended). I don't need a man to do these things. I CAN do them for myself or pay someone to do them for me. This revelation made me start questioning why I even needed him. Uh oh, it wasn't looking so good for the future of our relationship at this point.

Even though I was having these thoughts, our relationship continued on until he bought me a ring and asked me to marry him. The strange thing was, he still put the ring on my finger even though I never said yes. To make matters worse, a few days after his proposal, he admitted that he wasn't family-oriented. He only pretended to be family-oriented because he knew I would leave him, if I found out otherwise. Umm, yea! So, needless to say, I ended that relationship. And, yes, I gave the ring back… in case you were wondering.

Once I looked back at this relationship, I eventually realized that I had not written "family-oriented" on my then-forgotten list even though having someone in my life who was family-oriented was extremely important to me. But, more on this later.

Life Lesson #5: Never settle...No Matter How Good It Looks on Paper

Along came my second, long-term relationship and this one lasted about a year and half as well. It appeared that I was experiencing consistent luck with this online dating thing. This person hit almost all of the items I wanted on the then-forgotten list. But I eventually figured out that I forgot to write something else on my list.

Everything was going great! We got along, we were compatible, our kids liked each other, we liked each other's kids and his family instantly accepted us and made us feel at home. Ok, you might be thinking: This all sounds like it is going great, so what gives? Let me tell you, it was quite simple: HIS MOTHER! But you will need to hear the story to understand.

As things started progressing in our relationship, he started talking more and more about wanting us (the boys and I) to move in with him and he wanted to us to get married. But that was as far as it went! As we started spending more and more time together, it became evident that I wasn't the most important woman in his life.... His mother was! I know you might be thinking, come on, Wendi! She is the man's mother.

And, yes… I get that. But I just wasn't willing to deal with what that really meant.

He would call me several times a week stressing out because his mommy called him to give him a list of chores to do AT HIS OWN HOUSE. Keep in mind, this is a 40-something year old man. He would drone on and on about how he didn't want to do the things she was telling him to do, but he felt like he had to do them otherwise she would be upset. It had gotten to a point where I just couldn't take it anymore. I finally tried to explain to him that he was a grown-ass man and his mother shouldn't be telling him what chores to do nor did he need to listen to her. But he decided to ignore my advice and that, my friends, was the last straw! There can only be one queen of the castle… and honey, it's me.

This relationship taught me a very valuable lesson and that is to know what I wasn't willing to settle for… no matter how good it looked on paper.

Life Lesson #6: Some people are only meant to be in your life for a season

We all may have heard this life lesson talked about in one variation or another but no matter which version you have heard, it is true. Some people are only meant to be in your life for a season and the sooner you realize it, the better off you will be. This is where my third relationship from a dating app comes into play and this one lasted close to two years. Judging by the first date, I should have known that this one wasn't going to last.

On our first date, we decided that since both of us liked to dance that we should go to a dance club. So that's exactly what we did. As soon as we got there, we were out on the dance floor having a great time and then we decided to go grab a drink at the bar. And, that's where fate stepped in. As soon as I sat down at the bar, I instantly struck up a conversation with my now-friend, Debbie (who we will talk about a little later in this chapter) who happened to be sitting right next to me. I ended up talking to Debbie most of the night and I really didn't engage much with the guy I came with. That should have been a sign for myself or him, at least, to move on. But, noooo, I didn't take heed. He and I ended up living together and we had a lot of fun. We had so much in common. We liked to go dancing, go to concerts, and trying new restaurants and happy hours. This was great... I was having fun!

I have come to realize that this relationship came into my life when all I was really looking for was a companion. I was uber stressed out at work and I needed someone who I could just hang out with and be comfortable around. I needed a sense of status-quo in my life and he fit the bill.

Let's circle back for a moment to talk about the girl I met at the bar during our first date. Debbie and I became fast friends from the night I met her. Debbie has now become my Ride or Die. She will have my back no matter what and she will defend me to the death. She also happens to be very direct with everything she says. I am too...that's probably why we get along so well. She is the type of friend everyone wants and needs in their life.

Let's skip ahead to a couple of months later, Debbie came over to my house to hang out and drink some wine. This was the first time she had been around my then-boyfriend since the chance meeting at the bar several months before. She chatted politely for about 5 seconds then she went right for the jugular. She said to him, "Hi, I am Debbie. Remember me?" He nodded affirmatively. The next thing that came out of her mouth was, "You may have met her first, but I will still be here after you are gone." We all just laughed it off. But... she was right!

As time passed, Debbie would give me "gentle" reminders that I just wasn't that into him. But I wrestled with this thought because, quite frankly, I was comfortable, and I didn't feel like having to date again. When I finally couldn't shake the fact that

I didn't care for him in the way I should I have, I ended the relationship. From the beginning, I should have only kept him as a friend because deep down I knew from the first date that I didn't really want to be in a relationship with him. I also should have been brave enough to release him as soon as I knew, or should I say as soon as Debbie recognized that his season in my life was over.

As you can imagine, I was over everything at this point! I was struggling with the fact that I didn't want to have to date again but I didn't want to be alone forever either. It clearly was time to have another fire side chat with my friend, Charity. So, there we were, sitting around the fire, drinking our wine and I start singing the "woe is me" song. It sounded a little like this: I will never find anyone that is right for me… maybe I am supposed to be alone forever… the song goes on and on. I am sure you may have heard or even sang a version of this song at some point. Anyway, she then asked me if I looked at my list lately. I looked at her and asked, "What list?" Keep in mind, five years had gone by since I first wrote the list about what I was looking for in a partner and I tucked it away in my Bible. So, as soon as I got home, I pulled it out and read it. I immediately called her and read the list out loud. She said, "I can't believe this." Then she paused. I was confused so I asked her what she meant. She went on to say that she couldn't believe how good I was at manifesting. At the time, I had no clue what she meant by that. She went on to explain to me what manifesting was and how to do it. I was in disbelief until I really started thinking about the characteristics of the men that I had dated in comparison to the list I wrote.

I realized that these men had most of the characteristics that I was looking for in a partner. However, I also realized that there were several other important characteristics that they didn't have that I wanted to add to my list. That is when Charity convinced me to make a new list based on what I had learned from my past experiences. So, I started the process all over again. I wrote the new list (as seen in this book). I took out my old list and burned it. I then placed my new list in my Bible. Rest assured; we aren't done with the list just yet… we will come back to it in a later chapter.

INGREDIENT REFLECTION: Now, it is time for you to write the list of what you are looking for in a partner. Think hard about what is important to you while you write your list. Keep in mind: Your list can be as short or long as you want it to be.

Should I Take on Another Project?

The next two chapters aren't necessarily linked to online dating, but I couldn't write this book without talking about both of these topics. Let's jump right to it. Why do women always have the urge or think that we can fix someone? We need to learn to save ourselves from the inevitable headaches that are soon to follow when we try to do this.

We need to realize that we can't fix someone who doesn't want to be fixed nor should we even try. At this point in our lives, it doesn't matter if we are in our late 20's, 40's or 60's, we need to understand that a person will most likely be set in their ways. You shouldn't waste your precious time on trying to change him or her, particularly, if the issue is around a fundamental part of their personality or around the lack of something that you wish to change… period.

Life Lesson #7: When people show you who they are the first time, believe them

I think as the female species we are wired to second guess ourselves when it comes to this topic. We will come up with every excuse in the book to explain why he or she did this or that or why he or she said something in a certain way. We come up with these scenarios on what we think he or she really meant or how we can get them to do or say what we want to hear. I am guilty of doing this a time or two myself. However, all of my friends will tell you that I preach this to them all the time: When someone shows you who they are the first time, believe them. I have found that if you want to know what a man is thinking, just ask him and listen to what he ACTUALLY says... not what you think he said.

I know it is hard because we think we might be misinterpreting what they said or whatever else we make up in our head to support our delusion of what we want the outcome to be. Honey, we need to learn to let it go! The only way a person will change... is if they want to do it. And, no, you can't make them do it with sex, love, adoration or any other thing you can think of to add to the list. If they are not willing to give you what you need, move on. Trust me, you will find someone who will give you everything you have been longing for and more. Just hang in there a bit longer.

We are going to switch gears for a minute and talk about friends with benefits. This is a judgement-free zone here. If you are into this type of arrangement, great! If not, great! Either way, we need to talk about it for those who do or have been known to dabble in the friends with benefits arena. If this is your jam... GO FOR IT! I just want to remind you that this is a slippery slope. If you aren't careful, you could start to confuse yourself and the other person. In the beginning, you will both need to set clear boundaries on exactly what you are doing. This will help minimize someone from getting hurt, even though I will say someone usually does. You both should determine what works for your arrangement. Does that mean no sleeping in the same bed over night? No going out to restaurants? Whatever you decide, do it together and make sure everyone is on the same page.

Like I said before, the reason you do this is so that someone doesn't get hurt or start thinking they are in a "real" relationship when that is the furthest from the truth. I will apologize, in advance, because what I am getting ready to say is a little crude, but you can't turn a hoe into a househusband, ok? Sometimes we get into these situations thinking we can convince men that they want to be in a relationship with us and all we need to do is show him. Let me say this right now, NOOOOO... that isn't going to work. The reason why it won't work is exactly what I said a few paragraphs ago. If you want to know what a man wants, ASK HIM! So, if you are trying to go into this arrangement under false pretenses, trust me, it WILL blow up in your face!

INGREDIENT REFLECTION: Do you believe people when they show you who they are…the first time? If not, why do you think this is and how can you push yourself to change this behavior?

To Use Social Media or Not to Use Social Media?

Again, I don't think I would technically classify this chapter under lessons learned from online dating but it is still a valuable one nonetheless. News flash: I am about to get on my soapbox for a minute so just bear with me. This chapter talks about things that I have seen online that we, as women, need to stop doing ASAP. Don't get me wrong, I have been guilty of doing some of these things a time or two. But, please, for the love of God....STOP!!!

I am sure we have all heard the term, thirst posting. If you haven't, this is where someone continuously posts about wanting a boyfriend or husband or posting sexuality explicit photos trying to lure someone into a relationship with them.

Whatever you do, don't be that girl!

You really need to think about what these types of posts say about you. Let's be real, posting all of the memes and GIFs in the world aren't going to be enough to bring someone of value into your life nor will it make you feel any better in the long run. So, why waste your time posting these types of things?

Don't misunderstand what I am saying here. I am not trying to shame you about posting pictures of yourself in a bathing suit by the pool or the beach. I am saying if you are posting pictures of yourself or activities that you are doing just to see how many likes you can get or for "HIM" to see them... that's not the way to go about it. If you are out there living your best life or posting pictures of yourself because you are in the moment and enjoying your life...Great, do it! But, if it is for another reason, you might need to reconsider why you are doing it.

Life Lesson #8 - In time, what is meant for you will come

Those types of posts will have the opposite effect of what you are trying to accomplish or gain. So, learn to love yourself and have faith that what is meant for you will come in time. You don't have to try to force it. Enjoy being you and living your life to the fullest!

Moving on to the next part of this conversation…Let's imagine that someone is currently in a relationship that is falling apart and they are desperately trying to hold on to it. Can you guess what we see next on Facebook or Insta? All of these photos and comments about how in love they are or how they can't live without the other person, yada, yada. Yet, we all know that two days ago they posted, "Well, I am single again" or I don't need this or him or some other self-proclaimed statement of a new life. Come on now…. Save the drama and keep all that nonsense off of social media.

Again, I am not saying that you shouldn't post pictures of you and your honey biscuit. The point I am trying to get across here is that no one needs to know what happens behind closed doors. Leave it there!

Okay, rant over!

INGREDIENT REFLECTION: Take a look at your social media accounts. What do your posts say about you? Are you happy with it? If not, what are you going to change about what you choose to post?

I am Not the Marrying Type, or Am I?

Thank you for indulging me in that last two chapters, but I would have been remised if I hadn't brought those up. Okay, moving on to our next subject. This crazy roller coaster of online dating can have you questioning a lot of things about yourself. But it will also teach you some things along the way. So, hey… it isn't all that bad, right?!?

One of the things that I started to question about myself as I moved further along in my online dating journey was whether or not I was "the marrying type?" I had always thought I was so when I started thinking otherwise, it kind of threw me for a loop. As I told you before, I was in a long-term relationship during most of my youth and young adult life, so I just took it for face value that being "the marrying type" was just part of my DNA. As my experience with online dating ebbed and flowed, I started to really question this idea about myself. I mean, did I really even want to be "the marrying type" anymore? There were so many questions that I started thinking about.

Life Lesson #9: Growth isn't just about changing yourself; it is changing to make a better version of yourself

I started to think long and hard about how I had changed over the last several years and reflected on just how much I had learned about myself through this process.

The more I focused on my internal exploration, the more I discovered just how much I had grown as a person and understood exactly what I learned along the way. I learned:

- How to love myself for who I was (once I worked through my past emotions that held me back)
- How to be my authentic self (even though it was through trial and error)
- How to compromise (I was never really good at this in my younger years)
- How to accept others for who they are and not try to change them (this took me a little longer than I would like to admit)
- If I didn't love myself, I wouldn't be able to love anyone else (I had been told this before, but I had to figure it out on my own)

- How I showed love to others (Words of Affirmations and Physical Touch are my go-to ways to show others that I care for them. Thanks to the book, The 5 Love Languages)
- How I want to be shown love (Acts of Service is how I need to be shown love. Doing the little things goes a long way with me. Again, a big shout out to the book, The 5 Love Languages)

Ultimately, this internal exploration led me back to my original question, am I the marrying type? So, guess what I did next? Yep, you probably guessed it. I started making another list. But this time, it was a list of all the things I had to offer to someone.

The list of what I can offer to someone:
Loving
Stability
Loyalty
Dependable
Dedicated
Planner
Provider
Supportive
Faithful
Take Control
Fixer
Caring
Honest
Able to Cook
Family-Oriented
Straight-Forward

After composing my list and really thinking through each component, I realized that I did have a lot to offer to someone and that I was still truly open to the idea of marriage. Even though, somewhere or somehow along the way… I lost it. The only way I was able to find it again was to dig down deep and take an introspective look at myself to figure out what I had to offer to a partner and not focus only on what someone else could offer to me.

These were all powerful realizations. I would never have guessed all of these things would have come from clicking on a dating app. I can say without a doubt, that it took online dating to push me out of my comfort zone and challenge me in ways that I would have never expected. Once I started working on figuring out who I was, that is when I found myself on the path to finding the right person that would fulfill my life.

INGREDIENT REFLECTION: It is now time for you to make a list of the attributes you have to offer to a partner. Again, this can be as long or as short as you want it to be. This is for your eyes only.

How Do I Know When Someone Has Potential?

Earlier we discussed some of the crazy things that you may experience when you are dating online. What we didn't talk about was how to know when you found someone with real potential. Trust me, there are real, honorable men still out there. Do you have to kiss a lot of frogs to find him? Yes. Is it even worth it? Absolutely… so don't give up too soon!

The biggest piece of advice I can give you about this is something that you are going to want to ignore. You need to throw away (mentally, of course) whatever image or idea you have in your head of your ideal mate. You probably have some height requirement, preferred hair color or eye color and maybe even an overall body image of your dream man. You may have even considered what profession this imaginary man has. Now, that I have you thinking about your ideal man. Erase it now… completely!

You need to let go of any preconceived notions of what your dream partner looks like or does for a living in order to open yourself up to receive the person who is right for you… not the person you THINK will be right.

Now that we got that out of the way, let's talk about some things to look for when you start messaging with someone new. Disclaimer: I am not saying these are the MUST haves or are the only way for you to make the decision about moving this new person into the "maybe" column. I am saying that these are some of the things you should consider as orange flags (that is what I call them). These orange flags are signs that mean to move cautiously as he has passed through the first level of consideration.

Please understand that these flags cover the very basic things to look for. It is the first step in knowing that a person is looking at you in a way that is more than skin deep. Yes, I understand that you must be physically attracted to someone as a baseline but come on... that takes like 3.5 seconds to determine. You want to know that he took the time to read your profile and ask questions about who you are and what you wrote.

Here is a list of Orange Flags (this is not an exhaustive list):

- He uses your name in the salutation- Not babe, hun or some other annoyingly generic reference.
- He spells your name correctly- That's a must. First impressions matter, so he should take the time to learn how to spell your name correctly.
- He should know how to use proper grammar- He should know how to use your, you're and you are properly in a sentence.
- He leaves the ball in your court to respond- You shouldn't feel forced or guilted into responding back to him. If you do get that vibe, end it quickly.

Now, once you move this person further along into the "maybe" column you may be wondering…okay, what do I look for next? This stage is what I consider yellow flags.

Here is a list of Yellow Flags (this is not an exhaustive list):

- He doesn't ghost you- You know what I am talking about here… A man that seems very engaged at first then all of a sudden. POOF… you only hear crickets from him for a few days or weeks. That, my friend, is a ghost. Stay clear of this one. On the other hand, the man who consistently reaches out and follows up like he says he is going to do is the one to keep your eye on.
- He genuinely seems interested in you- He wants to know about your well-being. He wants to know how you are feeling or how your day is going and seems genuinely interested in you.
- He wants to know what you are looking for in a relationship- He does not just ask the basic questions about your favorite color, what job you have or what hobbies you like to do in your spare time. He wants to know more than what the superficial questions can tell him about you. Don't get me wrong, your conversations will start out like this of course, but it should quickly move into a deeper line of questioning. He will want to truly know what you are looking for in a partner and what you want in a relationship.

Okay, so this person has made it to the final stage of consideration, and you are nervous about it. So, what are some things to look for when this happens? I am going to call these the green flags.

Here is the list of Green Flags (this is not an exhaustive list):

- Communication flows easily- The conversation will feel natural and will just flow without any awkwardness. Time will seem to fly by when you are talking with each other. You may even feel like you have known each other for a longer period when, in reality, you haven't known each other long at all.
- Desire to talk to one another- You will feel a strong desire to talk to this person and he will feel the same way. It may even be described as a craving to hear from this person.
- Feeling excited- You will be overcome with the feeling of excitedness to talk to him even though you may have never actually met in-person.
- Takes you out of your comfort zone- You may even find yourself doing things out of your comfort zone. Let's say that you have always been a texter. If someone happened to call you, you would wait for the phone to stop ringing and then text something like "Sorry I missed your call. Did you need something?" But now you find yourself wanting to talk on the phone with this person more than texting with them.

At this point, your new love interest has made it through the barrage of consideration, what to do next? First, let me say, I am not telling you to go out and marry this person now. What I am saying is that now you have a solid base to work from and then and only then will you be on firm footing to move forward with a relationship of your choosing.

Life Lesson #10: Trust your intuition

We have all heard that little voice inside ourselves gently guiding us one way or another. Sometimes it has been known to give us a real, strong kick in the gut too. I have mentioned that it has happened to me a couple of times throughout this book. This usually happens when that little voice is telling us something that we don't want to hear or do and we try to ignore it. But we shouldn't!

Let's move back to discuss what happens after the green flag stage that we talked about in the previous chapter. Okay, you have made the decision to start dating a new person that you deemed worthy of yourself. Congratulations! It was a journey to get to this point, but you are now satisfied with your decision. Let's say a few months or even a few years have gone by and your intuition starts nudging you. Maybe it's trying to tell you something is wrong or maybe something is no longer serving you in this relationship. This is your prompt to act. This could be as simple as sitting down and talking to your honey biscuit about something that is bothering you or how you feel ignored or whatever the dilemma is that you might be facing at that time. I cannot stress this enough… when you feel or hear that little voice, it is time to take action.

After you follow through with whatever conversation you needed to have… give your partner some time. Now, I can't tell you how much time you should give that person, only you can be the judge of that. The bottom line here is either something has changed, or it hasn't. At this point, you will need to make a decision. If things have changed for the better… great! If things haven't changed, this is where the hard part begins. You will need to decide whether it is right for you to move on or not. Trust me, you will know what you need to do because that little voice will come around (perhaps a little too often) to remind you. This is your opportunity to stop and reflect on what you need to take from this season and look ahead to what is to come. Because you never know what might be waiting around the corner when the time is right.

INGREDIENT REFLECTION: Think about what items you would add to the flag lists above and classify them under the appropriate flag color: Orange, Yellow or Green based on your preferences.

Fairytale Endings.... Do They Exist?

Most of us probably grew up watching some version of a cartoon princess movie where she was just sitting around waiting for her knight in shining armor to come save her from whatever discombobulated mess the story plot had her in, right? As we got older, maybe our attention turned more toward the rom-com movie genre... where you always knew that no matter what twist of events occurred, the leading couple would always find a way to be together in the end. If this sounds even vaguely familiar, please understand that we have been set up (basically since birth) for failure when it comes to dating and marriage. We were programmed to expect these unrealistic dating and marriage narratives to unfold in our own lives (in one version or another). I mean, seriously, these movies never do go into all the trials and turbulations that are inevitability going to pop up once you open yourself up to dating or marriage nor do they talk about all the internal work that one needs to be done in order to get ourselves ready for love.

With that being said, I am a big believer in self-awareness and self-reflection. I believe by exploring both of them, we can fully open ourselves up to a world of possibilities when it comes to dating and marriage that we didn't even think was possible.

Online dating will force you to look within yourself, if you are willing to pay attention to what you are being shown and grow as a person.

Throughout this book, I have given you the cliff notes version of my past experiences and relationships, so I want to be clear that I had to do a lot of work on myself to be ready for the type of love I am about to tell you about that I didn't even see coming. When I say a lot of work... let's just say that in the beginning, I wasn't the easiest person to date. I was set in my ways and had no interest in doing things any other way. I am telling you this to give context to the story that I am getting ready to tell you.

Life Lesson#11: If something doesn't work out the first time, don't be afraid to try it again

Do you remember the horror story I told you about the man who went out on his first online date EVER and his date tried to get him to move in with her and take care of her son? Well, you might have thought that after he had that experience, it would have made him give up on dating online altogether, right? Nope... he didn't let that experience scare him away. Can you guess who his second date was with? You probably guessed it... it was ME!

Let me start by telling you his side of the story. He told me that he looked at my profile over and over again before he decided to reach out to me. He told me that he was looking for things not to line up in my profile story and for grammatical errors (which I am surprised he didn't find any because I surely didn't check it). After reading my profile multiple times and, by multiple times, he means a minimum of a dozen times. He finally reached out to me. Side note: I am a firm believer in letting the man make the first move. And, yes, I know many jaws may have dropped while reading this because I am an alpha female in every way. But there are some things I still believe a man should do first: a man should always make the first move whether it is in-person or online, a man should open doors for his woman and he should tell her that she is beautiful every day even if she hasn't showered in three days and her hair is matted to her head. I cannot confirm nor deny if I have ever been in this particular situation! LOL

Ok now, it's my turn to add to the story. He reached out to me on a Sunday afternoon and we started messaging within the app. We talked about our pasts, what we were looking for, what we liked and disliked. We talked about our kids and all the other things you would expect me to say at this point. Then, we quickly moved to texting (the next day). After a couple hours of texting, he asked if he could call me. Wait, what? Did he just ask if he could call me? I reluctantly agreed. And that's when it took off for us.

We spent hours and hours on the phone. This was all a bit of a foreign concept to me because 1) I had never had anyone ask if they could call me before and 2) I wasn't used to talking on the phone to anyone for long durations of time. Time seemed to fly by while we were talking on the phone. I mean we spent hours and hours talking on the phone before we even met in-person. The funny thing was that neither one of us even liked talking on the phone.

Fast forward to our fifth day of conversation (two days before our first date), we were talking on the phone and I jokingly asked if he googled me yet? He said no but hold on. He literally googled me while we were on the phone. I am going to give you a major piece of advice here. NEVER ASK THIS QUESTION!!!! Keep in mind, he is not very technologically savvy. The next words out of his mouth just about made me fall out of my chair.... He literally was able to provide me with my exact address and then went on to describe what my house looked like down to what structures were in my backyard. Eeekkkk!!! At this point, I am full-on hyperventilating. Again, I REPEAT... NEVER ASK SOMEONE THIS QUESTION. I mean it worked out for me in the long run, but it was not a smart thing to do.

Moving on, we went on our first, actual date two days later and it lasted SEVEN hours. The conversation was effortless, and we really gelled in every way. And even after we parted ways, we talked for three more hours before we went to bed. But, let me tell you something, as I closed the door after he dropped me off.... I knew I was going to marry that man. I could not believe I even uttered those words to myself. I started talking to myself... Wendi, get a grip, you can't be serious.... After one date? Yeah, I was serious...my little voice told me so!

Life Lesson #12: Don't give up on your fairytale

The next day, I told my aunt Kim and my friend, Charity, about the revelation that I had come to the night before. They both thought I had lost my damn mind. Quite frankly, I don't think either one of them could even wrap their head around the idea because I was usually so quick to dismiss dates for one reason or another. But it didn't matter to me what they or anyone else thought because I knew deep down that he was who I was always meant to be with.

Fast forward to after he asked me to marry him and I started telling people about it. The list of responses I received were along these lines: you have to be kidding…YOU, getting married?... I don't believe you… hell has frozen over. I mean even my boss told me and other colleagues…No way is she going to get married… It is just not going to happen…. And, he repeatedly made these statements. Long story short, we were married a year later and we couldn't be happier. He says that he had been waiting on me his entire life and I feel same way about him.

From the moment we started talking, it felt like we had known each other our entire lives. After the first date, we both knew we were meant to be together. Not to mention, he also had all of the characteristics I was looking for that I had on my list. Over the years, I have heard others explain similar things happening to them when they met the ONE, but I always thought they were making it up or exaggerating it a great deal. But let me tell you, they were not exaggerating AT ALL. This was exactly how I experienced it too when I met the ONE for me.

INGREDIENT REFLECTION: Pause and think about what your fairytale looks like. Not what the "who" looks like but focus on what your life would look like in your fairytale ending. Also, take note of what emotions you feel when you think about it. Remember to jot those down too!

What Coochie Wash Do You Use?

Yes, you read the title of this book and chapter right! This was the question asked to me by my friend, Debbie and, ultimately, prompted me to write this book. You remember my friend Debbie, right? She was my ride or die friend that I told you about earlier. Debbie and I were sitting out on my back deck drinking some wine and just chit chatting about what had been happening in our lives since we last spoke. The whole time she was here, she just watched how I was being treated by my husband. He treats me like a queen even though he will deny this because he says he is only treating me the way I deserve to be treated. Out of the blue, in her own Debbie-way… she asks, "What cootchie wash do you use?" I busted out laughing and asked her what in the world she was talking about. She said, "Girl, this man does everything for you. You need to share your secrets or at least tell me what cootchie wash you use!"

Ha! Is there some magical cootchie wash that we can buy that makes men treat us the way we should be treated? Boy, I wish there was. But we all know that this isn't something you can just go buy at your local drug store. There is a way to make your own version of cootchie wash, but it isn't what you have in mind. You have been writing the ingredients that make up your own personal cootchie wash as you have been working your way through this book. Let me explain.

Life Lesson #13: Know your worth.

If you have been writing down your ingredient reflections after each chapter of the book, you have been working on your final cootchie wash recipe. You have been adding new ingredients each time your internal exploration took you to a deeper level of understanding who you are and what you truly are looking for.

You created lists and questioned characteristics about yourself and others that helped you clarify what you truly want and deserve in life. Over time, you may even go back to your lists and notice that you have changed even more and that's okay. You are constantly learning and growing into a newer, better version of yourself. Each step of the way you have become more self-aware and closer to understanding what you truly desire and now you have a better picture of what your "fairytale" is.

Hopefully, you were also able to take some of these life lessons to heart to help you along your journey. The last two pieces of advice that I want to leave you with are: Don't give up, your perfect match is out there… just give it time. And, you never know when life is going to bring you exactly what you have been looking for. But rest assured… it will be when you least expect it!

Made in the USA
Monee, IL
04 November 2026

67379691R00039